Good company in a journey makes the way seem the shorter.
— IZAAK WALTON *(1593–1683)*
English biographer

The Traveler's Journal

*A personal notebook
— for travels real & imaginary*

From whatever place I write you will expect that part of my 'Travels' will consist of excursions in my own mind.

— S. T. COLERIDGE *(1772–1834)*
English writer

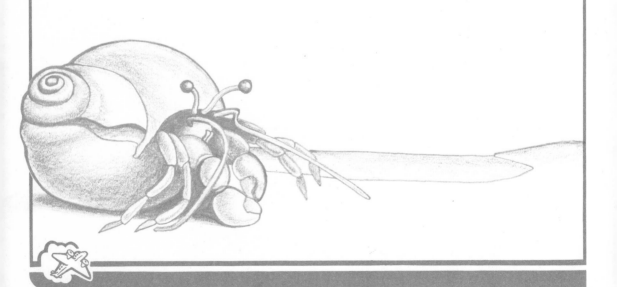

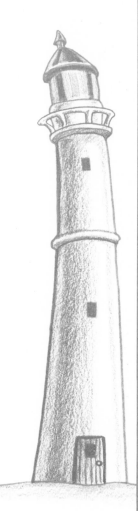

The traveler sees what he sees; the tripper sees what he has come to see.

— G. K. CHESTERTON *(1874–1936)*
English writer

Don't confuse your travel agent with God.

— KENNETH R. MORGAN, *b. 1916*
American writer

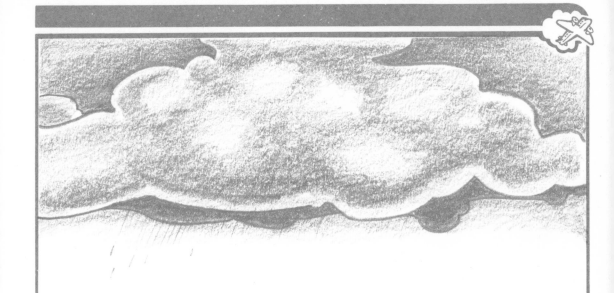

The only aspect of our travels that is guaranteed to hold an audience is disaster.

— MARTHA GELLMAN, b. 1908
American writer

The vagabond, when rich, is called a tourist.

— PAUL RICHARD, *b. 1939*
American writer

Three kinds of people die poor: those who divorce, those who incur debts, and those who move around too much.

— SENEGALESE PROVERB

The next best thing to being rich is travelling as though you were.
— STEPHEN BIRNBAUM, *b. 1937*
American editor and writer

All saints can do miracles, but few of them can keep a hotel.

— MARK TWAIN *(1835–1910)*
American writer

When we went on family trips, my uncle, Uncle Jimmy, would insist on, absolutely require, a window seat in the car. He just loved to watch the scenery go by. It got so his 'I got the window!' was the rallying cry for our extra-urban travels.

— MICHAEL MCCURDY, b. 1950
American philosopher

There are two kinds of travel—first class and with children.
— ROBERT BENCHLEY *(1899–1945)*
American humorist

. . . The little festive atmosphere of strangeness, of excitment, that only a holiday bedroom brings. This is ours for the moment, but no more. While we are in it we bring it life. When we have gone it no longer exists, it fades into anonymity.

— DAPHNE DU MAURIER, *b. 1907*
English writer

For some ill-defined reason, lovers have a particular penchant for travelling, perhaps in the hope that by exchanging backdrops for that of the unknown, those fleeting dreams will be retained a little longer.

— CAROLE CHESTER, *b. 1937*
English writer

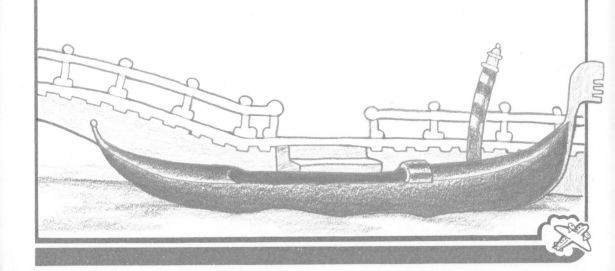

The traveller must be born again on the road, and earn a passport from the elements.

— HENRY DAVID THOREAU *(1817–1862)*
American writer

It has been my belief that in times of great stress, such as a four day vacation, the thin veneer of family unity wears off almost at once, and we are revealed in our true personalities.

— SHIRLEY JACKSON *(1920–1965)*
American writer

I often tire of myself and I have a notion that by travel I can add to my personality and so change myself a little.

— W. SOMERSET MAUGHAM *(1874–1965)*
English novellist

Here I am, safely returned over those peaks from a journey far more beautiful and strange than anything I had hoped for or imagined—how is it that this safe return brings such regret?

— PETER MATTHIESSEN, *b. 1927*
American writer

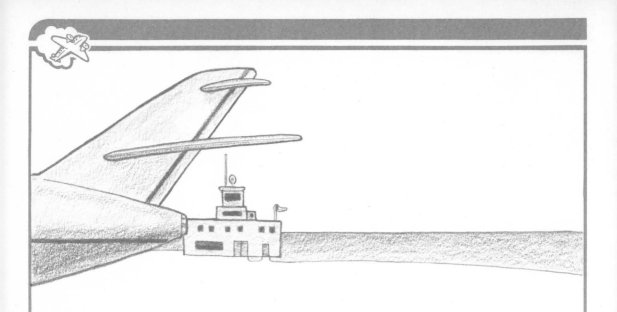

Is there anything as horrible as starting on a trip? Once you're off, that's all right, but the last moments are earthquake and convulsion, and the feeling that you are a snail being pulled off your rock.

— ANNE MORROW LINDBERGH, *b. 1906*
American writer

On a long journey even a straw weighs heavy.

— SPANISH PROVERB

The border means more than a customs house, a passport officer, a man with a gun. Over there everything is going to be different; life is never going to be quite the same again after your passport has been stamped.

— GRAHAM GREENE, *b. 1904*
British writer

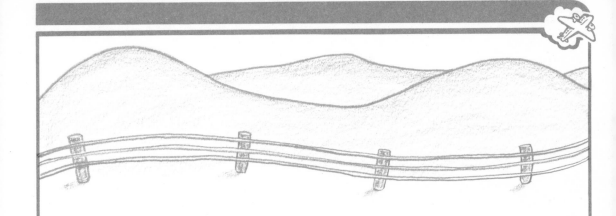

Someone said to Socrates that a certain man had grown no better by his travels. "I should think not," he said; "he took himself along with him."

— MICHEL DE MONTAIGNE (1533–1592)
French writer

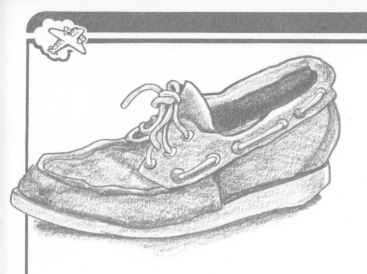

It is better to wear out one's shoes than one's sheets.

— GENOESE PROVERB

The day on which one starts out is not the time to start one's preparations.

— NIGERIAN PROVERB

Travel is the most private of pleasures. There is no greater bore than the travel bore. We do not in the least want to hear what he has seen in Hong-Kong.

— VITA SACKVILLE-WEST *(1892–1962)*
English writer

Travel is fatal to prejudice, bigotry, and narrow-mindedness.
— MARK TWAIN *(1835–1910)*
American author

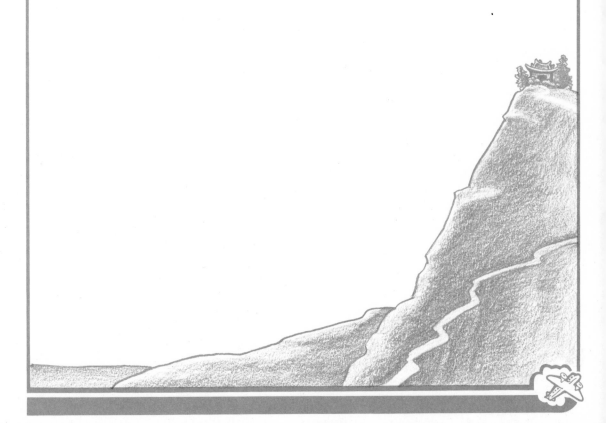

I never travel without my diary. One should always have something sensational to read in the train.

— OSCAR WILDE *(1856–1900)*
Irish playwright

Methods of locomotion have improved greatly in recent years, but places to go remain about the same.

— DON HEROLD *(1905–1960)*
American writer

A vacation is a period of increased and pleasurable activity when your wife is at the seashore.

— ELBERT HUBBURD, *b. 1927*
American writer

"Go West," said Horace Greeley, but my slogan is "Go Anyplace."

— RICHARD BISSELL *(1913–1981)*
American author

Traveling in the company of those we love is home in motion.
— LEIGH HUNT *(1784–1859)*
English writer

The car has become a secular sanctuary for the individual, his shrine to the self, his mobile Waldon Pond.

— EDWARD MCDONAGH, *b. 1922*
American journalist

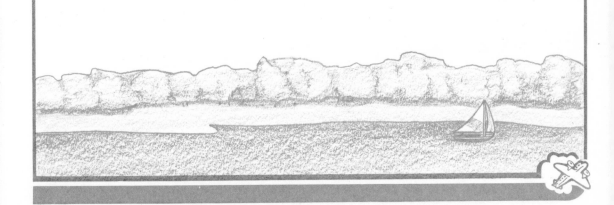

We may discover that a place does not become more interesting the farther away it is from the place we're in.

— ROBERT THOMAS ALLEN, *b. 1947*
American writer

*Travelling and freedom are perfect partners and offer an opportunity
to grow in new dimentions.*

— DONNA GOLDFEIN, *b. 1933*
American Writer

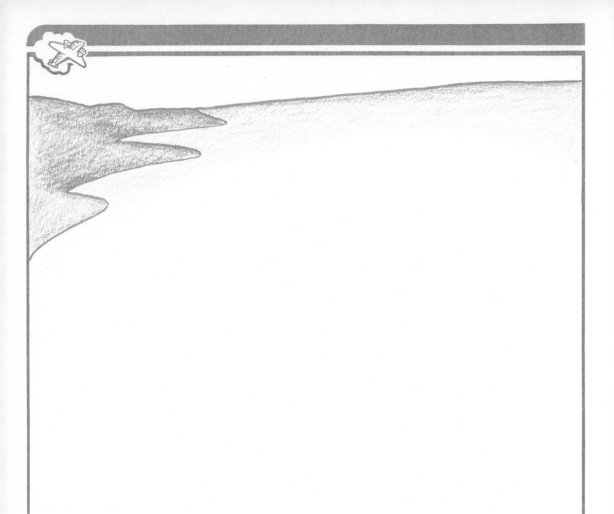

Those who go overseas find a change of climate, not a change of soul.

— HORACE *(65 B.C.–8 B.C.)*
Roman poet and satirist

A wise traveler never despises his own country.

— CARLO GOLDONI *(1707–1793)*
Italian dramatist

Every land has its own special rhythm, and unless the traveler takes the time to learn the rhythm, he or she will remain an outsider there always.

— JULIETTE DE BAIRCLI LEVY, *b. 1937*
English writer

Some of them seemed possessed of an incorrigible inner urge simply to take off and explore, to use whatever excuse was necessary to travel into country where no one else had been, to see where the rivers went, to find a pass through a mountain range that no one else had crossed.

— DAVID THOMPSON, *b. 1938*
American writer

The Soul of a journey is liberty, perfect liberty, to think, feel, do just as one pleases.

— WILLIAM HAZLITT *(1778–1830)*
English writer

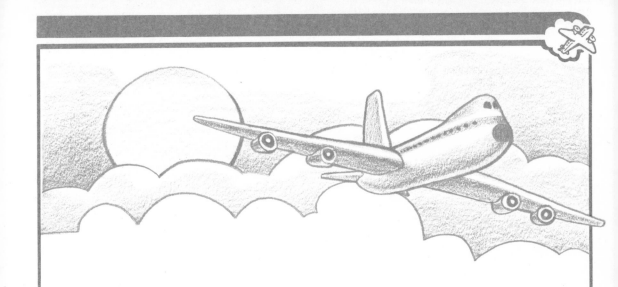

Though a plane is not the ideal place really to think, to reassess or reevaluate things, it is a great place to have the illusion of doing so, and often the illusion will suffice.

— SHANA ALEXANDER, *b. 1925*
American journalist

Too often travel, instead of broadening the mind, merely lengthens the conversation.

— ELIZABETH DREW, *b. 1935*
American writer

Road, n. A strip of land over which one may pass from where it is too tiresome to be to where it is too futile to go.

— AMBROSE BIERCE *(1842–1914)*
American writer

Everything in life is somewhere else, and you get there in a car.
— E.B. WHITE, *b. 1899*
American writer

Throughout history it has been man who worships and polishes the vehicle, and woman who packs the suitcases.

— JOHN FOWLES, *b. 1926*
American writer

The traveler was active: he went strenuously in search of people, of adventure, of experience. The tourist is passive: he expects interesting things to happen to him. He goes "sight-seeing."

— DANIEL J. BOORSTIN, *b. 1919*
American writer

People travel to faraway places to watch, in fascination, the kind of people they ignore at home.

— DAGOBERT D. RUNES, *b. 1902*
American writer

She travels grubbiest who travels light.

— ERMA BOMBECK, *b. 1927*
Humor columnist

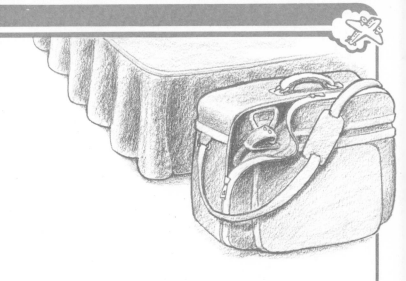

Above all, remember that the most important thing you can take anywhere is not a Gucci bag or French-cut jeans; it's an open mind.

— GAIL RUBIN BERENY, *b. 1942*
American author

Keeping to the main road is easy, but people love to be sidetracked.
— LAO TZU *(570 B.C.–490 B.C.)*
Chinese philosopher

One always begins to forgive a place as soon as it's left behind.
— CHARLES DICKENS *(1812–1870)*
English writer

A vacation is what you take when you can no longer take what you've been taking.

— EARL WILSON, *b. 1907*
American writer

Remember: don't start conversations with strangers on a trip. No way of getting rid of them later!

— ISIDORA AGUIRRE, *b. 1922*
Chilean playwright

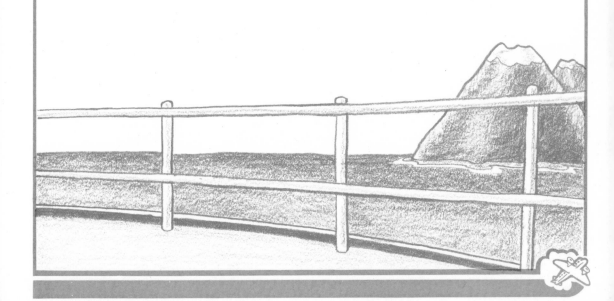

Most of my treasured memories of travel are recollections of sitting.
— ROBERT THOMAS ALLEN, *b. 1947*
American writer

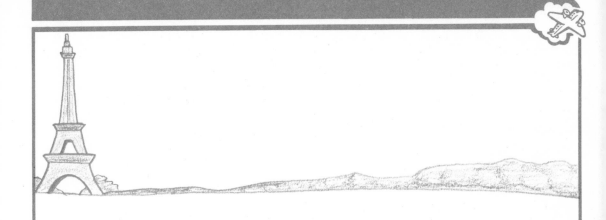

Holidays are enticing for the first week or so. After that, it is no longer such a novelty to rise late and have little to do.

— MARGARET LAURENCE, *b. 1926*
Canadian writer

I am sure that no traveler seeing things through author's spectacles can see them as they are. . . .

— HARRIET MARTINEAU *(1802–1876)*
English writer

Keep things on your trip in perspective, and you'll be amazed at the perspective you'll gain on things back home while you're away. . . . One's little world is put into perspective by the bigger world out there.

— GAIL RUBIN BERENY, *b. 1942*
American writer

We will travel as far as we can, but we cannot in one lifetime see all that we would see or learn all that we hunger to know.

— LOREN EISELEY *(1907–1977)*
American anthropologist

Women have always yearned for faraway places. It was no accident that a woman financed the first package tour of the New World, and you can bet Isabella would have taken the trip herself, only Ferdinand wouldn't let her go.

— ROSLYN FRIEDMAN, *b. 1924*
American writer

There are three wants which can never be satisfied: that of the rich, who wants something more; that of the sick, who wants something different, and that of the traveller, who says "Anywhere but here."

— RALPH WALDO EMERSON *(1803–1882)*
American essayist and writer

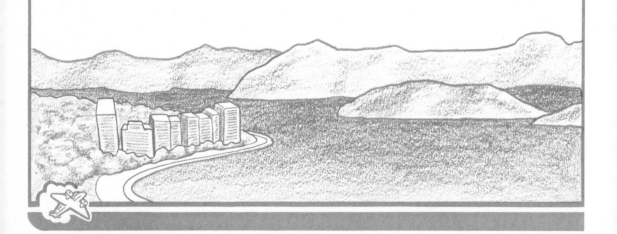

He who is everywhere is nowhere.

— SENECA *(4 B.C.–A.D. 65)*
Roman statesman and tragedian

*"What place would you advise me to visit now?" he asked.
"The planet Earth," replied the geographer. "It has a good
reputation."*

— ANTOINE DE SAINT EXUPÉRY *(1900–1944)*
French author

I was once asked if I'd like to meet the president of a certain country. I said, "No. But I'd love to meet some sheepherders." The sheepherders, farmers and taxi drivers are often the most fascinating people.

— JAMES MICHENER, *b. 1907*
American author

A journey is a person in itself; no two are alike. And all plans, safeguards, policies and coercion are fruitless. We find after years of struggle that we do not take a trip; a trip takes us.

— JOHN STEINBECK *(1902–1968)*
American author

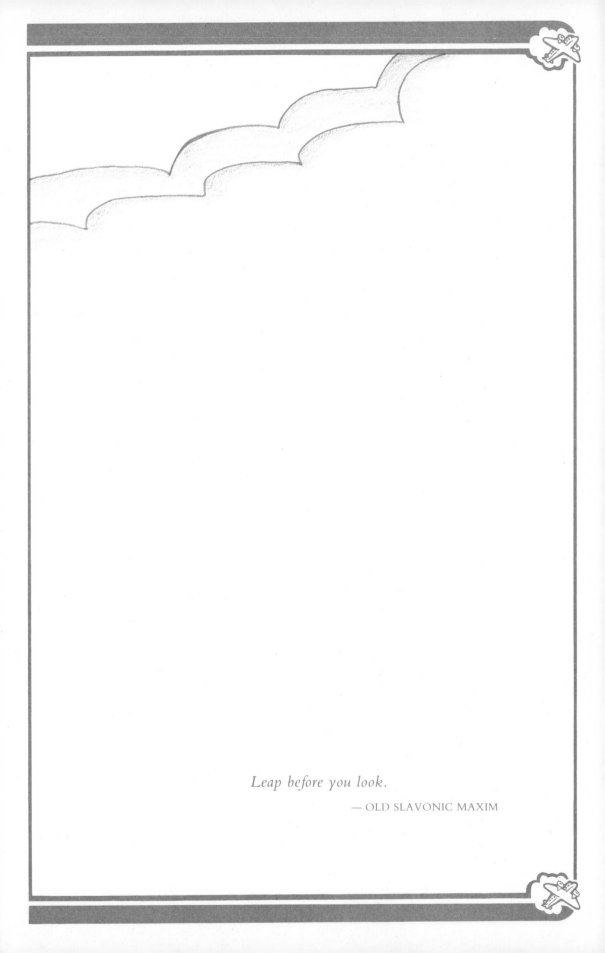

Leap before you look.

— OLD SLAVONIC MAXIM

Never journey without something to eat in your pocket. If only to throw to dogs when attacked by them.

— E. S. BATES *(1879–1939)*
American writer

The wise man travels to discover himself.
— JAMES RUSSELL LOWELL *(1819–1891)*
American poet

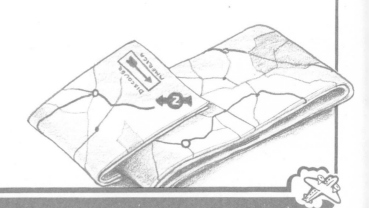

The journey not the arrival matters.

— T. S. ELIOT *(1888–1965)*
American-born English poet

Mileage craziness is a serious condition that exists in many forms. It can hit unsuspecting travelers while driving cars, motorcycles, riding in planes, crossing the country on bicycles or on foot. The symptoms may lead to obsessively placing more importance on how many miles are traveled than on the real reason for traveling.

— PETER JENKINS, *b. 1951*
American writer

If you don't like museums at all here, why go to them somewhere else?

— GAIL RUBIN BERENY, *b. 1946*
American writer

A traveller is one who travels many miles to have his picture snapped in front of statues.

— MAX GRALNICK, *b. 1929*
American writer

A good walker leaves no tracks.
— LAO TZU *(570 B.C.–490 B.C.)*
  Chinese philosopher

It is better to travel alone than with a bad companion.

— SENEGALESE PROVERB

I think there is a fatality in it—I seldom go to the place I set out for.

— L. STERNE *(1713–1768)*
English writer

If you live long enough, you'll see everything.

— TALMUD: PESAHIM, 113a

A travel adventure has no substitute. It is the ultimate experience, your one big opportunity for flair.

— ROSALIND MASSOW, *b. 1948*
American writer

We only need travel enough to give our intellects an airing.
— HENRY DAVID THOREAU, *(1817–1862)*
American poet, essayist and philosopher

I hoped that the trip would be the best of all journeys: a journey into ourselves.

— SHIRLEY MACLAINE, *b. 1934*
American actress

Voyaging is victory.

— ARAB PROVERB

When going by coach, avoid women, especially old women; they always want the best places.

— E.S. BATES *(1879–1939)*
American writer

Travel is travail.
— ARABIC PROVERB

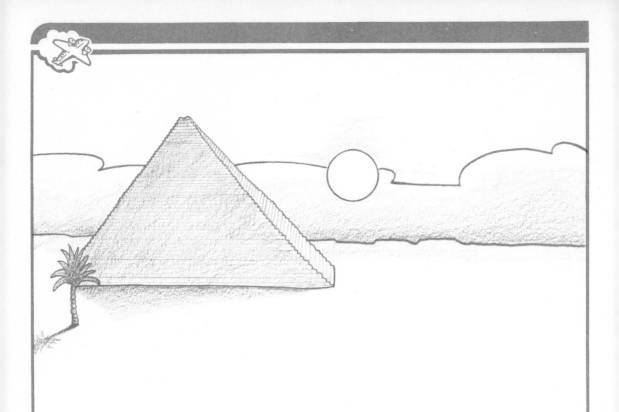

The further you go, the more you shall see and know.

— MEDIEVAL PROVERB

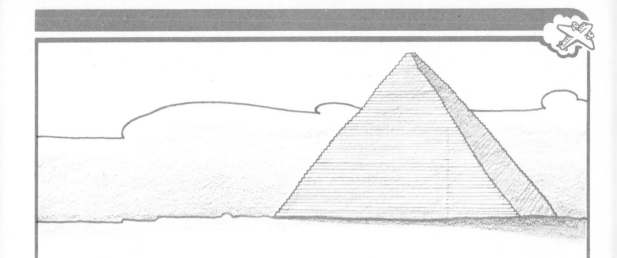

It is a strange thing to come home. While yet on the journey,
you cannot at all realize how strange it will be.

— SELMA LAGERLÖF *(1858–1940)*
Swedish writer (Nobel Winner)

Attitude, speech, and clothes differ as much from New York to Peoria as they do from Chicago to London.

— GAIL RUBIN BERENY, *b. 1942*
American writer

A good holiday is one spent among people whose notions of time are vaguer than yours.

— J. B. PRIESTLEY, *b. 1894*
British writer

A journey of a thousand miles starts under one's feet.

— LAO TZU *(570 B.C.–490 B.C.)*
Chinese philosopher

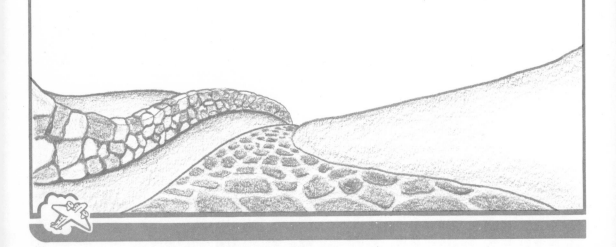

A traveler. I love his title. A traveler is to be reverenced as such.
His profession is the best symbol of our life. Going from—toward;
it is the history of every one of us.

— HENRY DAVID THOREAU *(1817–1862)*
American essayist

To look, really look out upon the world as it is framed in the window of a moving vehicle is to become a child again.

— ANONYMOUS *c. 1957*

The more the gypsy leaves your soul, the more the money stays in your pocket. Flexibility and independence cost money.

— GAIL RUBIN BERENY, *b. 1942*
American writer

The road to the city of Emeralds is paved with yellow brick.
— L. FRANK BAUM *(1856–1919)*
American writer

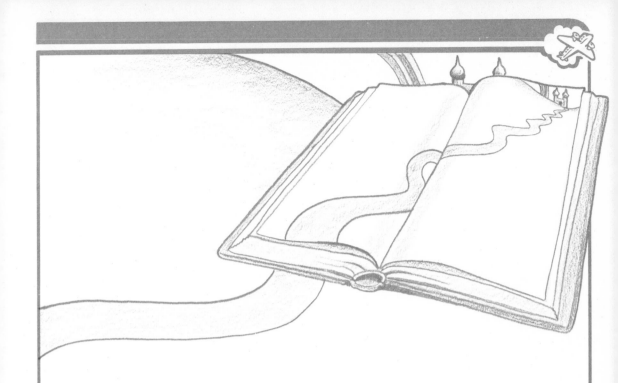

There is no frigate like a book
To take us lands away.

— EMILY DICKINSON *(1830–1886)*
American poet

Travelling may be . . . an experience we shall always remember, or an experience which, alas, we shall never forget.

— J. GORDON *(1896–1952)*
English writer

To know a foreign country at all you must not only have lived in it and in your own, but also in at least one other.

— W. SOMERSET MAUGHAM *(1874–1965)*
English writer

*A man can't stay relaxed too long, not under the best of circumstances,
and there's nothing like a trip with your family to prove my point.*
— MARRIJANE AND JOSEPH HAYES, *M—b. 1920; J—1918–1968*
American writers

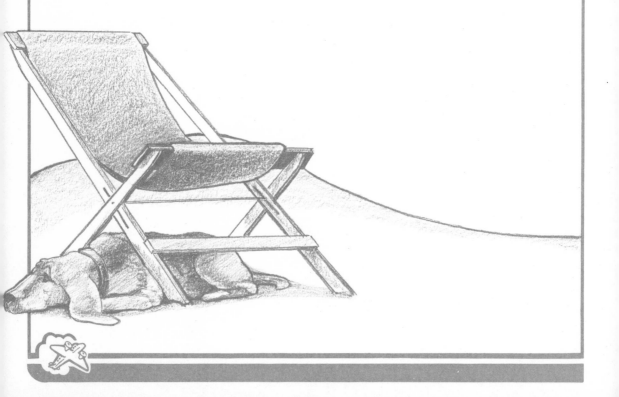

The good traveler has the gift of surprise.
— W. SOMERSET MAUGHAM *(1874–1965)*
English writer

From breakfast on through all the day
At home among my friends I stay,
But every night I go abroad
Afar into the land of Nod.

— ROBERT LOUIS STEVENSON *(1850–1894)*
Scottish novelist and poet